AMERICAN INDIAN ART AND CULTURE

The Ojibwa

MICHELLE LOMBERG

Go to www.av2books.com, and enter this book's unique code.

BOOK CODE

X948758

AV² by Weigl brings you media enhanced books that support active learning.

AV² provides enriched content that supplements and complements this book. Weigl's AV² books strive to create inspired learning and engage young minds in a total learning experience.

Your AV² Media Enhanced books come alive with...

Audio
Listen to sections of the book read aloud.

Key Words
Study vocabulary, and complete a matching word activity.

Video
Watch informative video clips.

Quizzes
Test your knowledge.

Embedded Weblinks
Gain additional information for research.

Slide Show
View images and captions, and prepare a presentation.

Try This!
Complete activities and hands-on experiments.

... and much, much more!

Published by AV² by Weigl
350 5th Avenue, 59th Floor
New York, NY 10118

Websites: www.av2books.com www.weigl.com

Library of Congress Cataloging-in-Publication Data
Lomberg, Michelle.
The Ojibwa / Michelle Lomberg.
pages cm. -- (American Indian art and culture)
Originally published: 2004.
Includes index.
ISBN 978-1-4896-2918-0 (hard cover : alk. paper) -- ISBN 978-1-4896-2919-7 (soft cover : alk. paper) -- ISBN 978-1-4896-2920-3 (single user ebook) -- ISBN 978-1-4896-2921-0 (multi-user ebook)
1. Ojibwa Indians--History--Juvenile literature. 2. Ojibwa Indians--Social life and customs--Juvenile literature. I. Title.
E99.C6L65 2014
977.004'97333--dc23
2014038978

Printed in the United States of America in Brainerd, Minnesota
1 2 3 4 5 6 7 8 9 18 17 16 15 14

122014
WEP051214

Project Coordinator: Heather Kissock
Design: Terry Paulhus

Every reasonable effort has been made to trace ownership and to obtain permission to reprint copyright material. The publishers would be pleased to have any errors or omissions brought to their attention so that they may be corrected in subsequent printings.

Weigl acknowledges Getty Images as its primary image supplier for this title.

Contents

AV² Book Code 2

The People 4

Ojibwa Homes 6

Ojibwa Communities 8

Ojibwa Clothing 10

Ojibwa Food 12

Tools, Weapons, and Defense 14

Ojibwa Religion 16

Ceremonies and Celebrations 18

Music and Dance 20

Language and Storytelling 22

Ojibwa Art 24

Ojibwa Creation 26

Studying the Ojibwa's Past 28

Quiz 30

Key Words/Index 31

Log on to www.av2books.com 32

The People

The Ojibwa are known by three names. Members of this American Indian group call themselves Ojibwa when speaking with people who are not part of their nation. When European settlers pronounced the word *Ojibwa,* they said *Chippewa*. As a result, the United States government calls this group the Chippewa. The name Chippewa is used in **treaties** and other official documents. The Ojibwa call themselves *Anishinaabe,* which means "first people."

In the 1600s, the Ojibwa began trading with French fur traders. They traded beaver skins for European goods, such as guns, cloth, beads, and metal. Soon, the Ojibwa **migrated** south and west. They moved closer to trading posts and areas where beavers were abundant.

Ojibwa traditions changed in each place. The Plains Ojibwa lived in northern North Dakota and Montana. Like other American Indians living in the Plains region, these groups depended on bison hunting to survive.

The Ojibwa are well known for their birchbark canoes.

The Woodlands Ojibwa included the southeastern and southwestern Ojibwa peoples. The southeastern Ojibwa lived in Michigan. They survived by hunting, fishing, and gathering. During the summer months, they also planted gardens, and harvested maple syrup and wild rice. The southwestern Ojibwa lived in Wisconsin and Minnesota. Wild rice was their main harvest. They were also gardeners, hunters, and fishermen.

OJIBWA MAP

Location of Ojibwa **reservations** in Minnesota

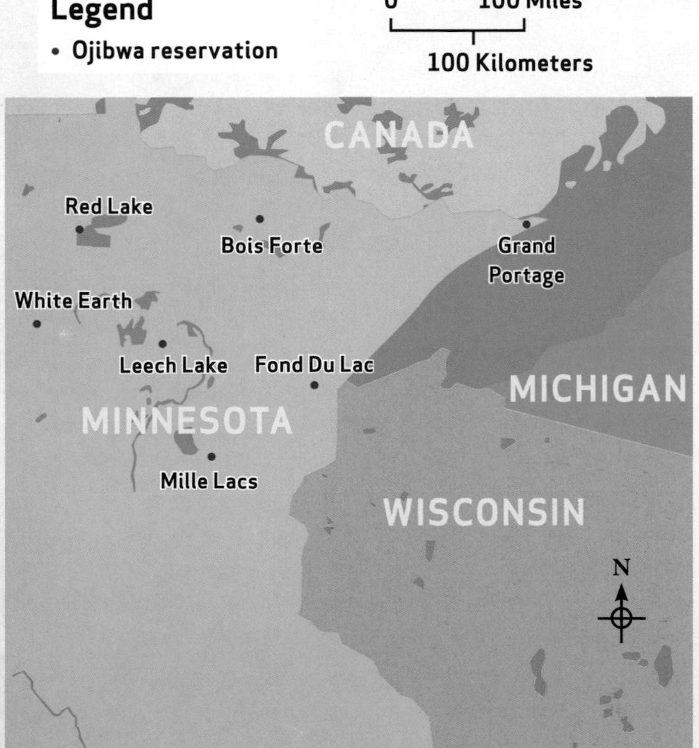

DID YOU KNOW?

Today, there are more than **100,000** Ojibwa living in the United States.

The Ojibwa signed ***more treaties*** with the U.S. government than any other American Indian group.

There are approximately **160,000** Ojibwa living in Canada today.

There are **20 Objibwa** reservations in the United States.

The Ojibwa were so involved in the **fur trade** in **Canada** that their language became the unofficial trade language.

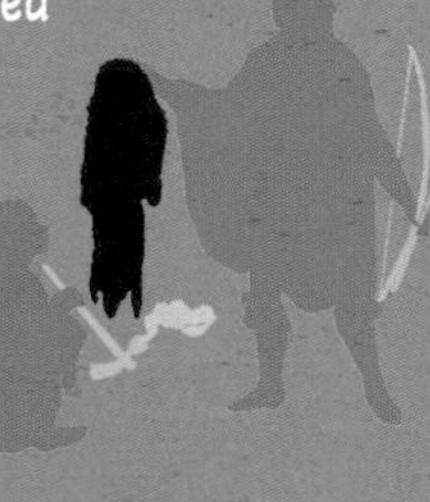

The Ojibwa **retained** the **rights** to **hunt, fish,** and **gather** plants on the land they sold to the **U.S. government.**

Ojibwa Homes

Traditionally, the Ojibwa lived in structures called wigwams. A wigwam was shaped like a dome. The Ojibwa built wigwams from materials they found in nature. They usually used wooden poles covered with **rush mats** and birchbark.

Ojibwa men and women worked together to build wigwams. First, the men set poles in the ground. Then, they bent the poles and tied them together to make a dome-shaped frame. Next, the women covered the frame with rush mats. They laid birchbark sheets over the mats. The birchbark sheets overlapped like shingles on a roof. This prevented rain and wind from entering the wigwam.

The Ojibwa moved several times a year to be close to food. When they moved, they left the frame of the wigwam, but took the birchbark strips and rush mats with them.

DWELLING AND DECORATION

Wigwams kept the Ojibwa warm and dry. A fire in the center of the wigwam provided heat and light. Smoke from the fire escaped through a hole in the top of the wigwam. A blanket, animal hide, or piece of birchbark covered the door. The floors of the wigwam were covered with cedar bark, rush mats, or branches. People sat and slept on mats and furs. Some wigwams had low platforms that served as seats and beds.

Today, the Ojibwa live in modern buildings on reservations and in cities and towns. They still build traditional structures for special ceremonies.

Traditionally, extended families made up of children, parents, and grandparents lived together in a wigwam.

Ojibwa Communities

Traditional Ojibwa life was loosely organized. A group of families that were related to each other was called a **clan**. Clans were named after their **totem** animals. Catfish, Crane, Bear, and Wolf are examples of clan names. Groups of people who were related through marriage were called bands. During the summer months, bands lived together in villages. In the winter, each family participated in a separate hunt. Some people, such as chiefs and **shamans**, held a high position in the community. However, most people were treated as equals.

Headmen, or chiefs, led bands of 300 to 400 people.

Over time, there have been many changes to Ojibwa culture. In the 1800s, much of the Ojibwa's traditional land was taken or bought by settlers. At that time, the U.S. government urged the Ojibwa and other American Indian groups to stop practicing their traditional ways of life. The Ojibwa were forced to end their **semi-nomadic** life and settle on reservations. Many Ojibwa left their reservations and moved to towns and cities after World War II.

Today, many Ojibwa still practice their traditional customs. In some areas of Michigan and Wisconsin, the Ojibwa continue to hunt and gather food. Some students preserve their culture by studying the Ojibwa language at community colleges. Today, there are about 44,000 native Ojibwa speakers.

In the Ojibwa belief system, wolves are the Ojibwa's relatives. Members of the Ojibwa community speak out against state-sanctioned wolf hunting and trapping.

MARRIAGE AND CHILDREN

A child who **misbehaved** had **charcoal** patted on its face.

Ojibwa girls played **"Butterfly Hide and Seek."** The seeker covered her eyes and sang, "Butterfly, butterfly, show me where to go," while the other girls hid.

A **young couple** spent the **first year of married life** living with the girl's family.

Ojibwa **girls got married at 14** or **15. Boys** could marry as soon as they could support a family through **hunting.**

Children were rarely scolded. **Adults used jokes, stories, and games** to teach good behavior.

Ojibwa Clothing

Long ago, the Ojibwa made clothing from materials they found in their surroundings. Most pieces were made from **buckskin**, the **tanned** hide of a deer. Among the Ojibwa who lived around Lake Superior, the men wore leggings, moccasins, and breechcloths. Breechcloths were similar to short pants. Women wore dresses, leggings, and moccasins. In the winter, the Ojibwa wore warm fur robes and mittens. Farther south, Ojibwa women wove fiber to make shirts. The women wore these shirts under sleeveless buckskin dresses.

Traditionally, women were responsible for making clothes. They began by tanning animal hides. First, they scraped the flesh and hair from the hides. Next, they washed the hides and rubbed them with animal brains to make them soft. The hides were then smoked to give them color. Women used tools made of wood and bone to cut and sew the hides.

Today, many Ojibwa wear store-bought clothes. However, they still wear some traditional garments. These include buckskin jackets.

Colorfully beaded moccasins and mittens are still popular among the Ojibwa people today.

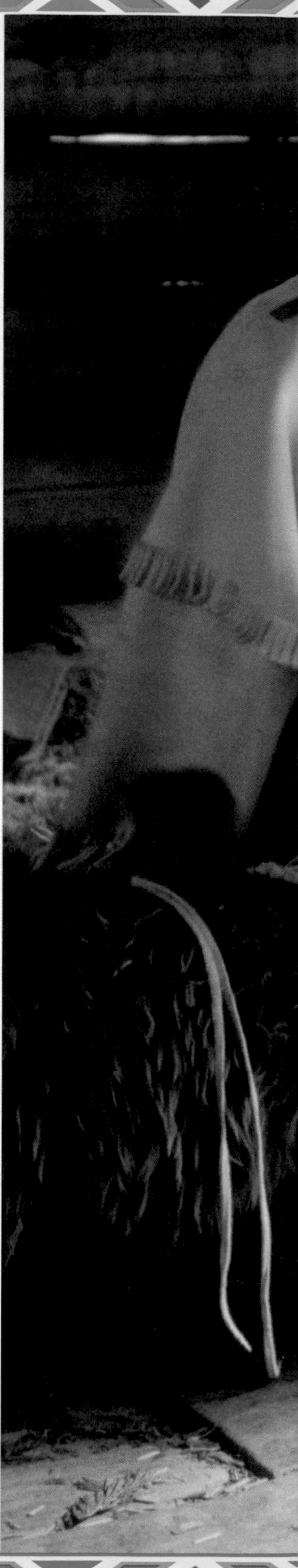

In the past, Ojibwa women used bone needles and thread made of plant fiber or animal sinew to sew buckskin clothes.

ADORNMENTS

Ojibwa women added detailed decorations to the clothes they made. They used plants to make blue, green, red, and yellow dyes. They used these dyes to color porcupine quills, which were added to clothing in elaborate patterns. European traders influenced the style of Ojibwa clothes. Women were able to obtain cloth, glass beads, buttons, and ribbon from the European traders. They used these items, along with traditional materials, to make clothes.

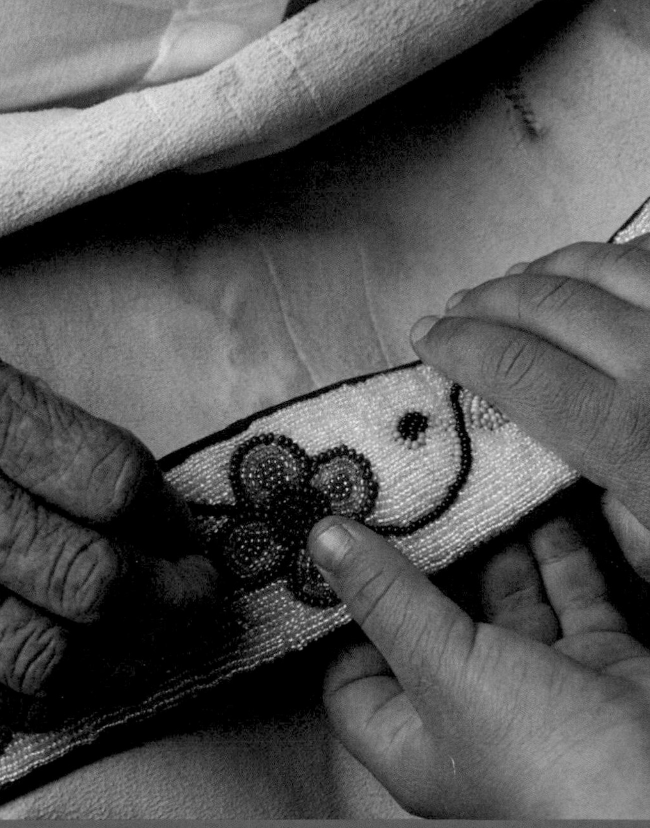

Ojibwa Food

Many Ojibwa groups ate a large variety of food. In warmer regions, Ojibwa women grew vegetables, such as beans, corn, and squash. Women and children also gathered berries. Ojibwa hunters and trappers provided their families with birds, fish, and meat. Meat was often roasted or boiled. Some meat was dried and mixed with fat and berries to make pemmican. Pemmican, which is similar to beef jerky, was a nutritious food that lasted a long time. Fish was an important food for the Ojibwa who lived around Lake Superior. Men caught fish with hooks, nets, and traps.

Wild rice was an important food for many Ojibwa. Wild rice is the seed of a grass that grows in shallow water. The rice was dried, boiled, and served with meat or fowl.

The Woodlands Ojibwa collected sap from maple trees to make sugar and syrup. The Plains Ojibwa did not have wild rice or maple sugar. Their main source of meat was bison. Bison meat was often made into pemmican.

To harvest wild rice, the Ojibwa paddle their canoes through the grass. They use sticks or paddles to knock the rice kernels into their canoes.

RECIPE

Popped Wild Rice

Ingredients:

- 2 to 3 tbsp. of corn oil or vegetable oil
- 1 cup of uncooked wild rice
- 1/4 cup melted butter
- 2 tbsp. of maple sugar or maple syrup
- salt to taste

Equipment:

- large bowl
- 12-inch skillet

Directions

1. Put the oil in the skillet.
2. With an adult's help, heat the oil on a stovetop at medium heat.
3. Add the rice to the skillet in a single layer.
4. With an adult's help, swirl the pan over the heat until most of the rice has popped.
5. Put the popped rice in a bowl.
6. Add butter, maple sugar, or maple syrup, and salt to the popped rice, and enjoy.

Tools, Weapons, and Defense

The Ojibwa used materials they found in their environment to make tools and shelter. Birchbark was an especially useful material for the Woodland Ojibwa. Women used birchbark to build wigwams. They also made birchbark bags and containers. Ojibwa men and women built birchbark canoes, too. These canoes were strong enough to use on fast-flowing rivers. The canoes were light enough to carry between rivers and lakes.

Tools made of other materials, such as bone and wood, were also important to the Ojibwa. Men used fishing hooks and lures made of bone or wood. Women used sharpened bones to scrape hides. They used **awls** and needles made of bone and wood to sew clothes.

In the 1600s, the Ojibwa began using metal items. They used guns, knives, and kettles for hunting, preparing food, and warfare. They traded with Europeans for these items.

Some Ojibwa craftspeople still hold the knowledge of how to make traditional birchbark containers and canoes.

HUNTING AND TRAVEL

Men used a variety of tools and techniques to hunt. Ojibwa hunters used blunt arrows to kill waterfowl. They caught small animals, such as rabbit, beaver, and otter, in **snares** or traps. They used larger **rawhide** snares to catch deer. Ojibwa men would also use traps made of sapling trees to trap deer. The hunter would drive the deer through the forest, into the traps.

The Ojibwa used special weapons during times of war. Ojibwa warriors often used a club. The war club was made of wood. It had a heavy, round knob on one end. Knives and bows and arrows were also used in the fighting.

The Ojibwa wore snowshoes when hunting or traveling in winter. Some Ojibwa snowshoes were rounded on both ends. Other Ojibwa snowshoes were long and narrow with upturned toes.

Snowshoes were made of wood, with strips of animal hide woven around the frames. This webbing allowed the wearer to walk across deep snow without sinking.

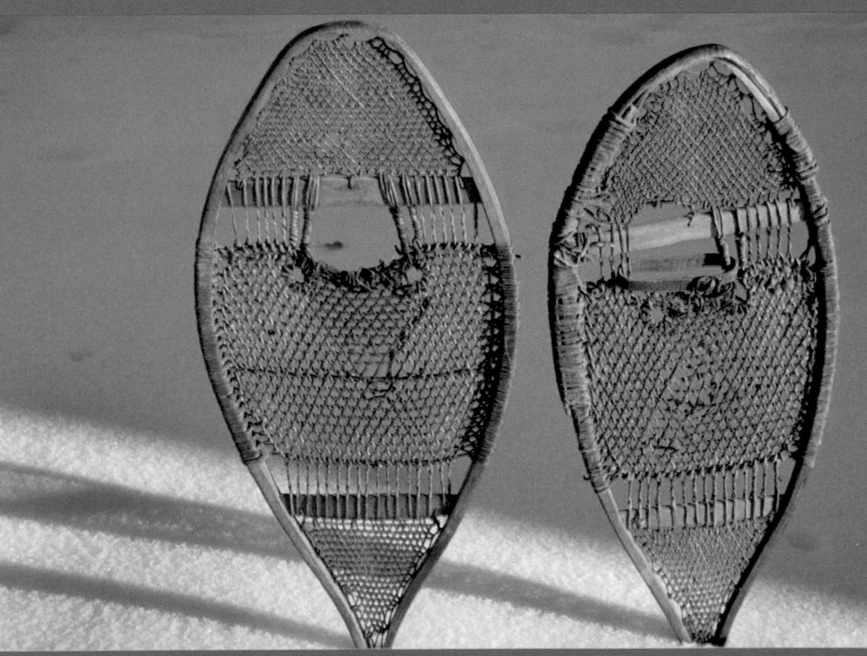

Ojibwa Religion

In traditional Ojibwa religion, the world was full of spirits. The Ojibwa called these spirits *manitous*. People tried to please the spirits by praying and offering tobacco. In return, the spirits provided good weather, animals to hunt, and bountiful harvests. Some Ojibwa groups believed in a creator called *Kitchi Manitou*, or Great Spirit.

The Ojibwa who lived around Lake Superior called the lake *Kitchigami*. Kitchigami was worshiped as a giver of life. Some spirits were not kind. Evil or angry spirits could bring illness and famine.

Ojibwa shamans were people with spiritual power. They gained this power during **vision quests**. Shamans were usually older men. They used their power to cure diseases brought on by evil spirits.

Ceremonial pipes were used for prayer and meditation.

The Midewiwin Society has been an important part of Ojibwa religion since the 1700s. It is also known as the Great Medicine Society. This society is devoted to curing illnesses and preserving old traditions. Members of the Midewiwin Society are leaders or healers who receive their healing power from the Great Spirit. Medicine men and women are called the *Mide*. The Mide invite people who appear to have healing powers to join the society. New members are taught to use plants for healing and how to conduct religious ceremonies.

Members of the Midewiwin Society sat according to a strict seating plan, which was recorded on birchbark.

OJIBWA BELIEFS

In Ojibwa religion, **birds** and **other animals** had a set of **rights**, such as the right to grow and multiply.

The Ojibwa held **animals** and **nature** in very **high regard**.

Young men spent several days in the forest alone without food, waiting for a **vision** of their special guardian spirit.

A prayer of **thanks** was given by the Ojibwa for every **animal** or **plant** they took **for food**.

The Ojibwa invented **dreamcatchers**. They were used as a charm to **protect** sleeping children from **nightmares**.

Ceremonies and Celebrations

The Ojibwa held many ceremonies and celebrations throughout the year. Springtime brought many reasons to celebrate. After spending the long winter apart, bands reunited to build summer villages. The maple sugar harvest was another holiday time. Families worked together to collect maple sap and prepare sugar.

Today, the Ojibwa and many other American Indian groups use celebrations called powwows as a time to gather and honor their culture.

The First Fruits ceremony took place during the wild rice harvest in late summer. The first rice grain harvested each season was offered to the Great Spirit. The rice grain was wrapped in tobacco leaves and placed in the water where it had been gathered. Then, the sweet **sage** spice was burned. The smoke from the burning sage carried a message of thanks to the Great Spirit.

Many years ago, the Ojibwa celebrated the Feast of the Dead. This feast was held every year. The Feast of the Dead was a time to remember and honor those who had died during the past year. It was also an opportunity for people from different villages to gather together. In addition to a feast, people enjoyed dancing, games, and contests. Guests received gifts from the host village.

Celebrations were also a time for playing sports. Lacrosse was a popular sport among Ojibwa men.

OJIBWA RECREATION

Ojibwa men enjoyed **games of chance.** They made dice from **animal bones.**

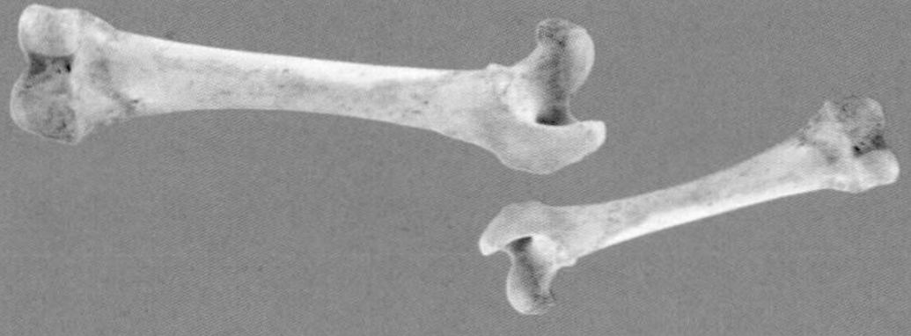

The Ojibwa had **games** for **adults** and games for **children.** Men and women played games **separately.**

Children played with **birchbark hoops.**

Women played a game similar to lacrosse called **double ball.**

The **snake game** was a game of chance played with **four sticks.**

Music and Dance

Music has always been important to the Ojibwa way of life. In ancient Ojibwa culture, songs were performed on many occasions. Some songs told stories to entertain children and adults. Others helped warriors prepare for battle. Healers sang to cure illnesses. Songs were also part of religious ceremonies.

The round shape of the drum symbolizes the circle of life.

The drum is an instrument used in Ojibwa music. Drums are made from wood and animal hide. The drum is seen as representing honesty, life, and sharing. Drums are always treated with great respect. The Drum Keeper is responsible for protecting the drum. He prevents people from reaching across a drum or using the drum as a table or chair.

Drums are usually surrounded by four or more singers.

CEREMONIAL DANCING

Dancing is another important part of Ojibwa culture. Usually, Ojibwa men and women perform traditional dances separately. Rattles and drums are used to create Ojibwa music. The dancers keep time to the beat of the drum. Some dances tell stories about war or hunting.

Today, Ojibwa people still enjoy traditional music and dances. People gather at powwows to display their song and dance skills. They compete in singing, dancing, and drumming contests.

The grass dance is a traditional Ojibwa dance. It is performed by males who wear clothes decorated with yarn or ribbon to represent long blades of grass.

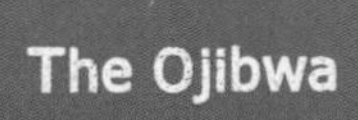

Language and Storytelling

The Ojibwa call their language *Anishinaabemowin*. This language belongs to the Algonquian **language family**. The Ojibwa language shares similar features with more than 30 other American Indian languages. Many of these languages are no longer spoken. Schools and colleges in several Ojibwa communities keep the Ojibwa language and traditions alive. There are many **dialects** of the Ojibwa language.

Ojibwa families used storytelling as a form of entertainment on long winter nights. Funny stories were told to amuse young children. Other stories were about the spirit world. Ancient tales were passed down from generation to generation. Storytellers also created stories about current events. The adventures of Nanabozho were popular subjects for stories. In Ojibwa **mythology**, Nanabozho was a hero who helped and protected people. He was also a trickster whose bad behavior often caused many problems.

Nanabozho is portrayed as a rabbit in some Ojibwa stories and is often referred to as the Great Rabbit.

PICTURES

Members of the Midewiwin Society used birchbark scrolls to record myths and rules for ceremonies. These scrolls served as memory aids for the shamans who had to remember songs, rituals, and recipes for healing medicines. The Ojibwa writing system did not contain an alphabet. Instead, the Ojibwa used pictographs to record information. These symbolic pictures were scratched onto birchbark sheets.

The Ojibwa sometimes drew pictures on rocks. They used **ochre** to draw or paint pictographs on rocks. Other times, pictures were carved onto rocks. These pictures are called petroglyphs.

Some petroglyphs represented dreams or visions of shamans and other Ojibwa people. For example, a young person on a vision quest might receive a dream name in his or her vision. This special name was never spoken out loud, but it could be recorded as a petroglyph.

Ojibwa pictographs included human and animal figures, spirits, and various shapes and patterns.

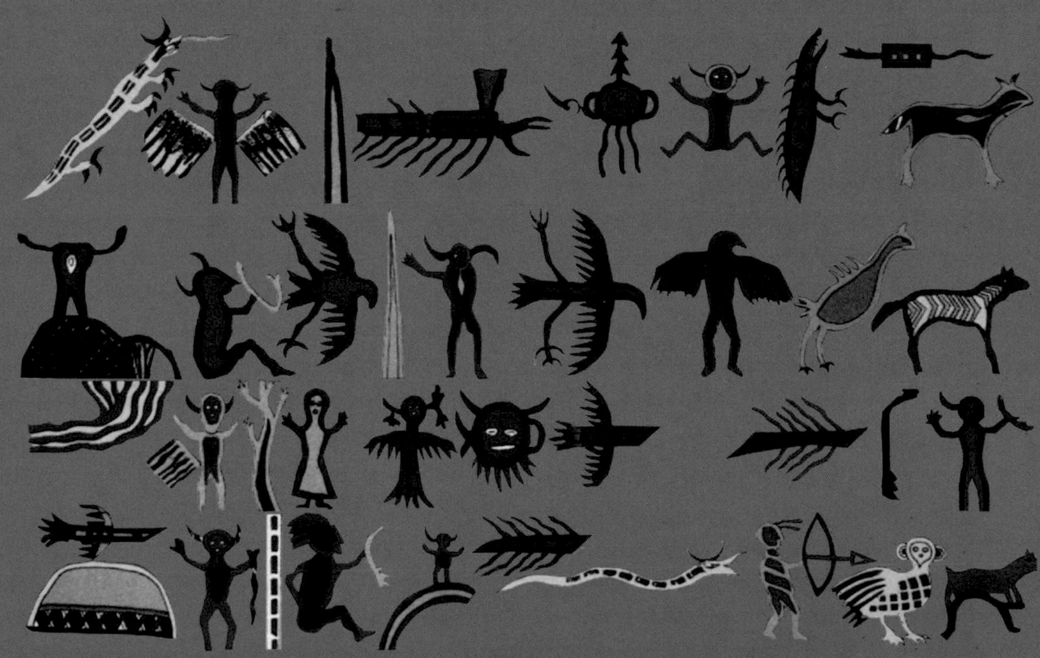

Ojibwa Art

Art was part of everyday life for the Ojibwa. Clothing, tools, and ceremonial items were finely crafted. Women decorated clothing, bags, baskets, and other objects with porcupine quills. Quills were plucked from a dead porcupine and sorted by size. The quills were dyed. Ojibwa women knew how to make bright dyes of blue, green, red, yellow, and black from local plants. Porcupine quills were used in a variety of ways. They could be woven or braided. They could be wrapped around wooden handles and pipe stems. They could even be threaded to make jewelry and belts.

The Ojibwa were also skilled weavers. Craftspeople wove strips of bark to create mats and bags. Different shades of bark created interesting patterns in the weaving. Ojibwa men were talented wood carvers. They created bowls, spoons, and other items. These pieces were often decorated with engraved figures.

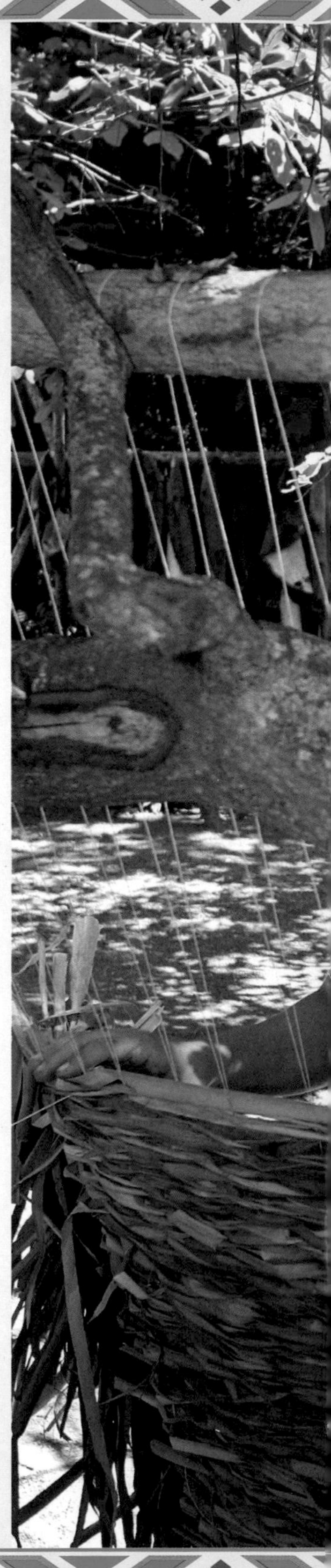

The Ojibwa still practice traditional arts and crafts. Woodcarving continues to be a craft enjoyed by many Ojibwa men.

Today, Ojibwa weavers and other craftspeople give public displays of traditional crafts.

BIRCHBARK

Birchbark biting is a unique art form that has been practiced by the Ojibwa for hundreds of years. The artist selects a paper-thin piece of birchbark that has no holes or marks. Carefully, the artist folds the birchbark and uses his or her fingernail to scratch a design onto the folded bark. Then, the artist uses his or her canine, or pointed, teeth to bite into the bark and trace the design. The tooth marks leave a delicate pattern when the bark is unfolded.

Ojibwa Creation

According to Ojibwa oral history, the world began with Mother Earth, Father Sky, Grandmother Moon, and Grandfather Sun. The Great Spirit took the four elements of earth, wind, fire, and water from Mother Earth. Using a sacred shell, the Great Spirit blew the breath of life into these elements. He created the first man, Nanabozho. The Great Spirit lowered Nanabozho to Earth.

Another story tells how the Ojibwa came to live around the Great Lakes. The story begins with the Great Spirit sending a crane to make its home on Earth. As it flew toward Earth, the bird gave a loud, echoing cry. The crane circled around the Great Lakes and let out a second cry. The crane was pleased with the clear water and many fish in the lakes. It decided to live on the Great Lakes. Again, it gave a loud, echoing cry. The people of the Bear Clan, Catfish Clan, Marten Clan, and Loon Clan heard the crane's call and gathered on the shores of the Great Lakes.

The crane is very important to the Ojibwa. It represents a position of influence.

There is also a story about the introduction of the clan system to the Ojibwa. According to the story, many years ago when the Ojibwa were living along the Atlantic Coast, seven spiritual beings appeared out of the ocean. Six of the spiritual beings remained on Earth to teach the Ojibwa how to live according to the clan system. The spiritual beings then returned to the ocean.

The clan system was created to care for the needs of the people. Each clan was known by its animal symbol, or totem. The animal totem symbolized the strength and duties of the clan. The clans worked together to achieve the goals of the nation. The seven original clans were Crane, Loon, Bear, Hoof, Marten, Bird, and Fish.

The sacred shell of the Ojibwa is the small, white cowry. As well as being sacred, cowrie shells were also used for trading.

CLAN SYSTEM

Today, the Ojibwa have more than **20 CLANS**, including the lynx, wolf, and moose clans.

Important chiefs were traditionally chosen from the **Crane** and **Loon** clans.

The **Fish clan** produced **teachers** and **scholars.**

The **Bear clan** was so large that it was **divided** into body parts such as the **head**, the **ribs**, and the **feet.**

Members of the **Bear Clan** were traditionally **warriors**, **police**, and **healers.** This is often still the case today.

Members of the **Hoof Clan** were seen as skilled at **settling disputes.**

STUDYING THE OJIBWA'S PAST

Archaeologists learn about the past by studying ancient **artifacts**. They have learned how the Ojibwa lived long ago by studying the sites of ancient villages. Archaeologists dig up the dirt at these sites in search of tools, weapons, food remains, and other objects. These items tell archaeologists how the Ojibwa hunted and fought. These items also help archaeologists understand traditional Ojibwa culture.

Archaeologists study pictographs to learn more about the Ojibwa of the past.

Timeline

Early Archaic Period

8000 B.C.—B.C. 6000
Early American Indians settled around the Great Lakes.

Middle Archaic Period

6000 B.C.—B.C. 3000

The Ojibwa settled around Lake Ojibwa, Wisconsin.

Middle Woodland Period

300 B.C.—A.D. 500

Mound Builder Peoples lived in the Upper Great Lakes region.

Late Woodland Period

500 A.D.—1620

The Ojibwa moved from the east coast to the Great Lakes region.

Oral histories are an important source of information about Ojibwa culture. These stories and legends are passed down from generation to generation. Ojibwa **elders** tell stories about traditional ways of life and past events. Recorded history also provides information about the Ojibwa's past. European explorers and traders observed Ojibwa culture. They recorded their observations. These records describe Ojibwa culture in the 1600s, when the Ojibwa first had contact with Europeans.

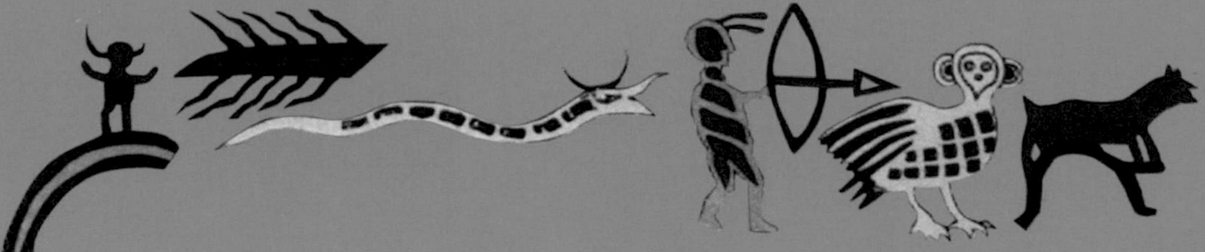

Elders help archaeologists understand pictographs and petroglyphs.

French Period

1620—1763

France controlled the Great Lakes region. The Ojibwa met European traders and missionaries. In 1660, the Ojibwa moved west, into the Mississippi Valley.

British Period

1763—1814

Great Britain gained control of the Upper Great Lakes. Pontiac, an Ojibwa warrior, led a rebellion against the British.

American Period

1814—present

The United States controlled the Great Lakes region south of Canada. The Ojibwa signed treaties with the U.S. government. Reservations were established in Michigan, Minnesota, and Wisconsin.

QUIZ

1 What name are the Ojibwa known by in treaties and other official documents?

A. Chippewa

2 In which Ojibwa dance performed by men do dancers wear clothes decorated with yarn or ribbon?

A. The grass dance

3 What kind of structure did the Ojibwa traditionally live in?

A. Wigwam

4 What name was given to a group of families that were related to each other?

A. Clan

5 In the past, what was most Ojibwa clothing made from?

A. Buckskin

6 Which natural material was used by the Woodlands Ojibwa for making wigwams, bags, containers, and canoes?

A. Birchbark

7 Which special item did the Ojibwa wear for hunting or traveling in winter?

A. Snowshoes

8 Which sport was traditionally popular among the Ojibwa?

A. Lacrosse

9 What food was particular to the Woodlands Ojibwa?

A. Maple sugar and syrup

10 In Ojibwa mythology, which hero helped and protected people?

A. Nanabozho

KEY WORDS

archaeologists: scientists who study objects from the past to learn about past civilizations

artifacts: objects made by humans

awls: sharp tools used for making holes in soft materials

buckskin: leather made from deerskin

clan: a group of families that were blood relatives

dialects: changes in a language that is spoken in a certain place

elders: older, influential members of a family or group

language family: a group of languages that share similar origin, grammar, and words

migrated: moved from one region to another in a large group

mythology: a set of traditional stories about ancient times or natural events

ochre: an earthy pigment varying from light yellow to brown or red

rawhide: untanned animal skin that has been allowed to harden

reservations: lands set apart by the federal government for a special purpose, especially for the use by an American Indian group

rush mats: mats made from branches of bull rush

sage: a plant with grayish-green leaves that is often used to flavor food

semi-nomadic: spending part of the year moving from place to place in search of animals to hunt

shamans: people with special spiritual powers

snares: traps that have a rope that tightens around small animals

tanned: animal hides made into leather

totem: an animal, plant, or natural object used as a symbol by American Indian clans

treaties: formal agreements between groups of people

vision quests: times of prayer seeking supernatural guidance

INDEX

archaeologists 28
art 23, 24, 25, 29

birchbark 4, 6, 7, 14, 23, 25, 30
birchbark biting 25
bison 4, 12

canoes 4, 12, 14
ceremonies 7, 17, 18, 19, 20, 21, 23
clothing 10, 11, 14, 24

dances 19, 21, 30
drums 20, 21

Feast of the Dead 19
First Fruits 19
food 4, 5, 9, 12, 13, 14, 17, 28, 30

games 19
gardens 5
grass dance 21
Great Lakes 26, 28, 29
Great Spirit 16, 17, 19, 26

hunting 4, 5, 8, 9, 14, 15, 16, 21, 28, 30

lacrosse 19, 30
language 9, 22

Midewiwin 17, 23
moccasins 10

Nanabozho 22, 26

petroglyphs 23, 29
pictographs 23, 29
powwows 18, 21

quill work 11, 24

religion 16, 17
reservations 5, 9, 29
rice 5, 12, 13, 19

shamans 8, 16, 23
songs 20, 21, 23
storytelling 22

tools 10, 11, 12, 14, 15, 24, 28

wigwams 6, 7, 14, 30

Log on to www.av2books.com

AV² by Weigl brings you media enhanced books that support active learning. Go to www.av2books.com, and enter the special code found on page 2 of this book. You will gain access to enriched and enhanced content that supplements and complements this book. Content includes video, audio, weblinks, quizzes, a slide show, and activities.

AV² Online Navigation

Audio
Listen to sections of the book read aloud.

Book Pages
AV² pages directly correspond to pages in the book.

Video
Watch informative video clips.

Embedded Weblinks
Gain additional information for research.

Key Words
Study vocabulary, and complete a matching word activity.

Try This!
Complete activities and hands-on experiments.

Quizzes
Test your knowledge.

Slide Show
View images and captions, and prepare a presentation.

AV² was built to bridge the gap between print and digital. We encourage you to tell us what you like and what you want to see in the future.

Sign up to be an AV² Ambassador at www.av2books.com/ambassador.

Due to the dynamic nature of the Internet, some of the URLs and activities provided as part of AV² by Weigl may have changed or ceased to exist. AV² by Weigl accepts no responsibility for any such changes. All media enhanced books are regularly monitored to update addresses and sites in a timely manner. Contact AV² by Weigl at 1-866-649-3445 or av2books@weigl.com with any questions, comments, or feedback.